Coaching at Work
A practical guide to help busy managers achieve results

First published 2012 by Hummingbird Effect
an imprint of Upfront Publishing of Peterborough, England.

www.fast-print.net/store.php

Coaching at Work : A Practical Guide to Help Busy
Managers Achieve Results
Copyright © Denise Collins 2012

ISBN: 978-178035-308-1

The right of Denise Collins to be identified as the author of this work has
been asserted by him in accordance with the Copyright, Designs and
Patents Act 1988 and any subsequent amendments thereto.

A catalogue record for this book is available from the British Library

An environmentally friendly book printed and bound in England by
www.printondemand-worldwide.com

This book is made entirely of chain-of-custody materials

– COACHING AT WORK –

A Practical Guide to help Busy Managers Achieve Results

– DENISE COLLINS –

Coaching at Work

A practical guide to help busy managers achieve results.

This book is for busy managers, leaders and all those who want to improve performance and maximize the potential of people.

It is for you if:

o   You are expected to coach others.

o   You are interested in discovering simple ways to develop your own potential.

o   Your role would be easier if your team members were more confident, competent and responsible, and had better problem solving and effective decision making skills.

o   This book offers a practical, no-nonsense, easy-to-apply-in-the-real-world guide to coaching.

Denise Collins

From this book you will gain:

★   Insight into and understanding of why you need to be coaching.

★   Confidence in knowing what skills a great coach has, and how you can easily develop them.

★   Competence in using frameworks and models which actually work in real-world situations.

★   The flexibility to handle the unexpected.

"These days most leaders and managers struggle to do everything that needs to be done in less time and with fewer resources.

Perhaps you find yourself searching for a better way to motivate and improve the performance of your team?

Maybe you wish the people who report to you were more competent, responsible, confident or better at problem solving and effective decision making?

If they were, this would allow you to get on with higher level strategic work, rather than getting sucked into operational tasks or micromanagement.

Maybe your professional role includes the expectation that you will coach, even if you have not been given sufficient guidance on how to actually do this successfully!

In this book I provide you with practical ways to develop the potential of your team using a coaching approach.

Why is this important to you?

Basically, because when your team looks good, you look great!

You don't have time to wade through heavy jargon and theory so in this book I offer practical, solid frameworks that are effective in real situations."

Regards

Denise

Looking for practical, professional, independently-approved training?

I f you:

* are looking to add skills that are significantly useful in both your professional and personal life,

* have an interest in a variety of ways to develop, support and help yourself and others,

* know a bit about NLP and/or coaching and want to know more,

* feel it is important to you to attend independently-approved useful training

then please check out The Hummingbird Effect open training programmes in:

Eclectic Life and Business Coaching

Recognized by The Association for Coaching and

Approved by The Institute of Leadership and Management as a Development Programme.

NLP Practitioner

Accredited by The Association for NLP

NLP Master Practitioner

Accredited by The Association for NLP

For up-to-date details and special offers visit
www.hummingbirdeffect.com

Looking for corporate training and development for your organization that continues to add value long after the event?

Visit www.hummingbirdeffect.com for information on:

Bespoke development programmes and the current range of in-house programmes including:

* Being an inspiring and effective leader

* Creating an effective coaching culture

* Practical coaching for managers

* Coaching at work, that works!

* Confidence, inside and out

* Presentation skills

* Time management

* Stress management

* The art of training

- ★ NLP at work

- ★ Enhancing customer service

- ★ Building more effective teams

Visit www.hummingbirdeffect.com

Or call:

01245 476376

Do you want to learn from your past, improve your present and create the future you truly desire?

Denise now works with only a select few clients on a one-to-one basis. Utilizing a synthesis of integrated therapeutic coaching and development approaches, she helps people to be the best they can be.

If you want to enhance what you already do well and identify, clarify and achieve what you want from your personal and professional life please get in touch to find out about her availability to see you on an individual basis.

Visit www.hummingbirdeffect.com to discover how individual consultancy can help you.

Or to speak with Denise call 01245 476376

Sincere Thanks

I would like to thank:

* ★ YOU for selecting this book. Without you reading it there would be little point in its existence!

* ★ all my clients, and the many and varied people who have attended my different training programmes over the years. You have all taught me so much.

* ★ my Dad, Thomas Kennett, who sadly passed away last year and never actually got to see me finish a book. (Although he saw me start lots!) Many years ago it was my Dad who gave me that initial push out of a lonely place of self-pity and into the brilliant world of self-development. Wherever he is now, he knows I love him, I miss him and I will always be thankful that he was my Dad.

* ★ my family for their unerring encouragement and support in my quest for my own self-improvement. Plus their understanding of my "workaholic" attitude to spending time developing the business I love so much.

★ Phoebe, for all the cups of tea and coffee while I was writing.

★ last but not least, Bella and Missy for being my ever faithful companions in the office!

About the author

Denise Collins MSc, BSc (Hons) is founder and principal of The Hummingbird Effect personal and professional development consultancy, based in Chelmsford, Essex.

Denise has been a psychological coach in private practice for 12 years. Since 2005 she has been designing and delivering both open training courses and in-house programmes.

Denise is highly respected and regarded as a professional in the "self-development and improvement arena". However, her understanding is not merely theoretical. Born into a working class family in South East London, she left school with few formal qualifications. She was married for the first time at 18, had her first child at 20 and was a single parent living on state benefits by the age of 21. Miserable, unfulfilled and feeling as if she had failed to reach her potential she was prompted by her father to "stop feeling sorry for herself" and "go and do an evening class or something!" As a result she started an enduring love affair with education, self-improvement and overcoming adversity which led her to go back to study for a degree (being the first person in her family to achieve this).

Her qualifications include; an MSc in Coaching from The University of East London, an upper second class honours BSc degree in Social Sciences from South Bank University, an RSA teaching & learning in adult education, an Open University management studies certificate. She is an NLP practitioner, NLP master practitioner and NLP trainer, certified by NLP co-creator John Grinder and accredited by the ANLP. In addition to academic qualifications, Denise has extensive knowledge and practical experience.

Denise is married to John. In 2011 they celebrated their silver wedding anniversary. They share a home in Chelmsford Essex with their two retired greyhounds.

Denise is the proud mother of three wonderful grown-up offspring, Jacob, Phoebe and Liam. And Grandma to the fabulous Ruby and the "bump" who is expected to make an appearance in summer 2012.

Coaching.

An introduction to what it is. And what it isn't.

Sir John Whitmore who popularized the GROW coaching model said:

"A coach is not a problem solver, a teacher, an adviser, an instructor or even an expert; he or she is a sounding board, a facilitator, an awareness raiser."

Coaching is sometimes confused with other types of "talking solutions".

The following should provide a little clarity on the distinctions:

* A therapist will explore what is stopping you doing something.

* A counsellor will listen to your anxieties about doing something.

* A mentor will share tips from their experience of how they did something.

* A coach will encourage and support you in actually doing that something.

Coaching is not rocket science!

In my opinion a great deal of the information, training and books on the subject are guilty of over-complicating coaching to the point where it seems as if you require a university degree to undertake it as a management activity. (For your information I do, in fact, possess not just a degree, but a postgraduate Masters Degree in Coaching, and take it from me, you really don't need one to be an effective coach!)

Coaching could be defined as asking incisive questions that enable the development of solutions rather than providing direct information, advice or instruction. Coaching is about assisting someone to learn rather than teaching them.

Coaching is in fact quite a simple process.

However, "simple" should not be confused with being easy.

It is not easy to coach well.

One of the aims of this book is to offer an uncomplicated path for you as a manager to coach well.

The origin of the term "coach" derives from 15th century word for horse-drawn transport.

The symbolism that a coach takes people to where they want to be, is nicely appropriate.

A question for you…

If the people who report to you were more:

competent,

aware,

confident,

prepared to take responsibility for their actions,

able to make effective decisions and find solutions to problems,

would it make your job of managing them less stressful?

Well, coaching can help achieve all this.

During my experience of coaching individual managers, plus the research I undertook for my MSc in coaching psychology at The University of East London, I noticed that many stressed managers immediately resort to offering solutions, providing answers and even taking over responsibility for operational tasks. While this may solve a problem in the short term, in the longer term it merely adds to the managers' stress by increasing dependency upon them and reducing the confidence levels and competence of teams. This further increases managers' stress and personal workload.

There is a lot of evidence which concludes that managers who get the most out of their teams, spend a high proportion of their time and energy coaching. It is becoming increasingly common for managers to be expected to coach as a part of their role. Sometimes without any formal training or even clear instruction on what this actually entails or even how to actually do it.

Adopting a coaching approach can enhance the skills of those you manage and thereby reduce your stress.

Research has indicated that managers:

★ are often so busy "putting out fires" that they feel overwhelmed and therefore find it difficult to accomplish the strategic elements of their role.

★ frequently end up doing things themselves (even sometimes taking over operational tasks from direct reports) because they feel it is just easier and quicker than telling or showing someone else what needs to be done.

★ sometimes have little confidence in the competence and ability of staff to problem solve successfully or make effective decisions.

Coaching can help you...

Delegate more efficiently, improve productivity, communicate your message more clearly, conduct more effective developmental conversations, get better results in a shorter time, create a stronger sense of purpose within your team, successfully motivate the performance of others, spend less time fire-fighting or doing jobs that should be done by your direct reports, free up your time and expertise so you can focus on the most important tasks and enjoy greater satisfaction in your personal and professional life.

It has been proved that those who receive effective coaching develop increased awareness and are more prepared to take responsibility. In the longer term this develops qualities such as self-belief and confidence which actually leads to improvements in competence (in those being coached). And therefore a reduction in stress for the coaching manger.

The manager as coach

Having responsibility for other people's performance and results can be challenging. You have to delegate and supervise the work, but you also have to motivate people, build relationships, manage change, solve conflicts and deal with a host of other problems that the role of managing people effectively presents.

★ Managers who adopt a coaching approach get the work done and develop their people at the same time. This improves the quality of work and the quality of the working life. Managers with coaching skills have productive, honest relationships with their people where problems can be aired and innovative ideas shared.

★ Adopting a coaching approach can enhance both elements of the dual role of effective manager, to get the job done and develop people to fulfil their potential.

The shoelace principle

Adopting a coaching approach does require a bit of upfront investment. True, there are times when it can seem easier and quicker just to tell people what you want them to do, rather than utilizing the skills necessary to coach them. I call this "the shoelace principle". It may take a bit longer to teach a child how to tie her own shoelaces. However, if in an attempt to save time in the short term you continue to tie them for her, longer term this will become a liability. (Plus you will end up with adult offspring who are doomed to a lifetime of wearing slip-ons or shoes with Velcro fastenings.)

When coaching is not the best option

If a situation is a straightforward legitimate request for information or there is a crisis requiring immediate action then obviously to provide the information, undertake the task yourself, or give specific instructions on exactly what to do is probably fastest.

In all other management situations adopting a coaching approach will most likely improve the quality of the end result, lead to increased awareness, personal responsibility and generative improvement.

If you invest a little time developing the skills necessary to coach, there will be longer-term rewards for you as a manager. Acquiring coaching skills forms part of your own professional development enabling you to do the best job you can.

Coaching enables those you manage to develop or seek their own practical solutions to problems and sources of stress. Coaching offers a route to fully develop the potential of those you manage.

And let's face it, when your team look good, you as their manager look great!

A potted history of the origins of coaching

There are many influences and important developments that have contributed to what we now think of as coaching. Some of these crossed over. Some developed in different arenas simultaneously.

If you wanted to be literal about tracing the origins of coaching (that is asking questions that encourage the development of cognition) then you would probably have to go back to Socrates the ancient Greek philosopher. In a very small and simple nutshell, Socratic questioning covers the following:

★   Conceptual clarification

★   Probing assumptions

★   Exploring rationale, reasons, evidence

★   Questioning viewpoint and perspective

★   Investigating implications and consequences

★   Asking questions about the question

In 1937 Napoleon Hill wrote Think and Grow Rich a motivational self-help book about how to use the power of the mind to succeed in work and life.

In the 1950s, Norman Vincent Peale created what became a seminal work The Power of Positive Thinking. Expanding on key ideas such as: increasing self awareness; how we "filter" our experiences and build our expectations and assumptions about self; the world and other people; focusing on taking responsibility for our own actions and the notion that we have choice in our lives. These ideas may now be thought of as commonplace but were not always.

In 1975 Tim Gallwey wrote a book called The Inner Game of Tennis which is often referenced as shifting the focus for performance enhancement from instruction to the importance of internal mental processes in determining success, or otherwise.

In his book, Gallwey suggested that the opponent in one's head is greater than the one on the other side of the net. Basically, he described how limiting beliefs inhibit performance more than lack of ability or knowledge. The book proclaimed that unlocking people's potential to maximize their own performance was actually more important than acquiring technical skills.

It did not take too long for these ideas to migrate from sports coaching to the world of work. Gallwey went on to publish The Inner Game of Work. He also formed an association with John Whitmore, an English racing driver and sports coach. In 1992 Whitmore wrote Coaching for Performance. He developed perhaps the most influential model of coaching – the GROW model (originated by one of the founders of business and executive coaching, Graham Alexander).

With the advent of management and motivational theories, psychology began to play an increasingly important part in the world of business and work. Especially in the areas of understanding development needs, recruitment, selection and assessments procedures.

Stephen Covey's The Seven Habits of Highly Effective People is a groundbreaking book offering practical methods for improving personal and professional effectiveness which, although not strictly about coaching, is an important step on the road to the development of managerial coaching.

Neuro Linguistic Programming (NLP)

Originally developed in the 1970s at the University of Santa Cruz by Richard Bandler and John Grinder, NLP represents a practical methodology incorporating a variety of psychological concepts and techniques. NLP is utilized in many professional and personal domains, including management, sales and performance, interpersonal and communication skills, therapy and personal development, motivation and the utilization of effective learning techniques. Bandler and Grinder began by modelling the patterns of therapists: Milton Erickson, Gestalt therapist Fritz Perls and family therapist Virginia Satir. Since then, many others have contributed to the continued development of the field.

NLP has come to represent the study of excellence in any field of endeavour. NLP describes the modalities through which people interact with the world: visual, auditory and kinaesthetic. While NLP is a distinct discipline from coaching because it is essentially about communication, there are major areas of overlap. These include techniques to help build rapport, to "reframe" situations regarded as negative and to understand the potentially positive and negative effects of language such as presuppositions and generalizations.

Emotional Intelligence

In his 1995 book Emotional Intelligence American psychologist Daniel Goleman identified that IQ (Intelligence Quotient) is not the only, or perhaps even the predominant, indicator of success. Goleman suggests that self-awareness, self-discipline, persistence, altruism, personal motivation, empathy, and the ability to love and be loved by friends, partners and family members have a far more important role to play in human success than IQ. This Emotional Quotient (EQ) enables people to succeed in work as well as play, building thriving careers and healthy relationships. Goleman's model of what it means to be "intelligent".

There is now growing academic interest in psychological theoretical-based coaching models, e.g. cognitive behavioural coaching, which has its origins in cognitive behavioural therapy (CBT).

Some key ideas of CBT are:

★ Reality is subjective and exists in the mind of the individual. Adverse events obviously do occur but it is how we think and respond to events, rather than the events themselves, that can increase our difficulty in dealing with them. The viewpoint we choose and the meaning we give to events determines our reactions.

★ Negative or limiting beliefs about ourselves inhibit our ability to achieve. No matter how we acquire our negative beliefs, we continue to reinforce and strengthen those beliefs until we take active steps towards addressing them.

★ The best route to overcoming our limiting beliefs and bringing about emotional change (improving how we feel) is not by concentrating on our feelings but through cognitive change (how we think) and behavioural change (how we act).

Many of the tools and techniques offered to clients by coaches have their origins in CBT. These include: keeping a diary of events and associated feelings; questioning assumptions; evaluating unhelpful or unrealistic beliefs; trying out new ways of behaving and reacting, including using affirmations and visualizations.

Underpinning Skills

Okay you didn't get where you are today without being clever and knowledgeable,

but how intelligent are you?

I am talking about a specific type of intelligence.

To coach well requires skills that depend upon a degree of "Emotional Intelligence". The term "Emotional Intelligence" was originally developed during the 1970s and 1980s by psychologists Howard Gardner, Peter Salovey and John 'Jack' Mayer. In 1995 Daniel Goleman wrote his book which popularized the ideas.

Goleman identified five "domains" of EI:

*   Knowing your own emotions.

*   Managing your own emotions.

*   Being able to motivate yourself.

*   Recognizing and understanding the emotions of others.

*   Managing relationships, that is "managing" the emotions of others.

In a nutshell then, emotional intelligence is the ability:

★   to understand our own emotions (having self-awareness / knowing the emotional impact we have on others and the emotional impact others have on us.)

★   to appreciate the emotions of others (having empathy)

★   to manage our emotions and adapt our behaviour to achieve a mutually agreeable outcome.

How does this relate to coaching?

Coaching could be described as both an art and a science.

The science bit consists of the models and techniques we will focus on in more detail later in this book.

The art is in "not what you do, but how you do it!"

You could be the most knowledgeable coach on the planet in terms of the science, but if you are not capable of establishing and building relationships of mutual trust and understanding (the essence of rapport) your coaching is unlikely to reap the desired results.

Some deceptively simple ways to develop your EQ (emotional intelligence quotient)

★ Practise putting yourself in the position of others. Imagine being able to see situations from their perspective. How do you look to them? How do they perceive you? What do they read as your emotion? What impact do you have on them? How are they feeling? What are they thinking? What do they want? What is the world like for them? It is important to realize this is not intended to make them right and you wrong. It is simply to expand your ability to understand emotions and perceptions.

★ Practise noticing your own emotional state and how it impacts on your behaviour. Simply taking the time to notice how you are feeling and what behaviour this leads to will expand your self-awareness.

★ Notice how particular people or situations "make you feel". Or to be more accurate, how you respond in terms of your thoughts and feelings to certain external stimuli. Again, this self-awareness will lead to greater insight and understanding of yourself which results in more behavioural choice.

★ Once you are familiar with doing the above you will have much greater choice and control over how you act, react and behave. In NLP there is an idea taken from cybernetics, known as the law of requisite variety, that suggests an element (e.g. person) that can exhibit the greatest level of flexibility will eventually control the system. How useful is that in terms of management and leadership?

Six key abilities of the successful coach.

As coaching is primarily a planned developmental type of communication rather than natural or random conversation, the following are a solid foundation for the effective underpinning communication skills required to coach well:

1. Fully attending to the person being coached. Being "present" in terms of attention to verbal and non-verbal communication, e.g. body language, facial expressions, tone etc. without interpretation or judgment of what these may mean.

2. Active listening. In everyday interactions often we merely pause while the other person is talking, waiting until it is our turn to talk. Active listening includes reflecting back what has been said and the perceived meanings, summarizing and using empathy.

3. Ability to both support and challenge. Providing positive feedback and being encouragingly affirming is an essential element of coaching. However, to ensure that coaching does not become just a backslapping exercise or

cosy chat, the ability to challenge while maintaining rapport is also crucial.

4.   Ability to resist the temptation to tell / advise / instruct, even if you think you have the "perfect" answer. Coaching is about drawing out what the coachee has inside, rather than putting in information or instructions.

5.   Ability to motivate. The goals and outcomes identified during coaching will not be enough to create change without action. Motivation to action often relies upon the goal or outcome being important and meaningful and being within the grasp of the person being coached.

6.   Ability to ask relevant, incisive and open questions.

Elements of more empathetic communication are:

1.   Don't pretend not to notice emotions. Recognize their presence.

2.   Take a moment to imagine what the other person might be thinking or how they might be feeling.

3.   Be open with your perception of what they might be feeling. For example, "I can imagine

that must be…" or "It sounds like you're really upset about…".

4. Acknowledge their right to what they are feeling: "I totally understand why you are feeling…".

5. Respect their efforts to cope with the situation: "I appreciate that you have already tried… and now you have taken the step to…".

6. Offer support. For example, "I'm committed to helping you to…" or "Let's see what we can do together to…".

Those who are considered to have good people skills or be great communicators will often do the above, either consciously or unconsciously.

Ever thought how the human mind is a bit like a search engine?

When you search for something on the Internet the relevance of the results or quality of the information you get is largely dictated by the precision of the question posed.

In a way, the human mind works in a similar fashion. Certain types of questions point us in certain directions to find the answers.

If you ask "Why can't you do anything right?" the resulting answer will probably come back as some sort of excuse, where blame is placed firmly outside of self.

However, asking something like "How could we learn from this experience and improve the outcome next time?" provides the opportunity for a non-judgemental exploration of the current situation and sets the tone and direction towards positive advancement.

"Why did you do that?!" will prompt a very different answer to "What are the facts and what needs to be done to improve the situation?"

A question that elicits an "I can't" or "I don't know" type of response is likely to halt the internal mental search for an answer altogether.

Our use of language not only describes human experience, it actually plays a part in creating it. Our thoughts will be guided in a certain direction in response to a question. An effective coach must develop a conscious awareness about their use of language. This is because the phrasing of questions and the impact of words influences the quality of the coaching.

"Whether you think you can, or whether you think you can't, you're probably right."

Henry Ford

I think this is a fantastic quote which has relevance to coaching on many levels. There has been research which indicates that the attitude and expectation of a coach will have an impact on the level of success, or otherwise, of their coachee. Basically, whatever you believe about your coachee's ability is likely to become a self-fulfilling prophecy. When coaching others it is vital that you presuppose success. That way you will think and talk in the direction of the desired outcome. An example of this kind of presupposing success would be to say something like, "When you achieve your goal..." rather than using the word "If". Positive expectancy is more likely to result in resourceful and flexible communication and behaviour.

> *"Success is the ability to go from failure to failure without losing your enthusiasm."*

> *Winston Churchill*

Okay, so I'm putting this quote here with a little tongue in cheek attitude. Of course the intention is to learn from "failures" so as not to repeat the same mistakes. Indeed, one of the best known presuppositions of NLP is "There is no such thing as failure, only feedback!" Meaning as long as we do learn from experience and adjust our behaviour accordingly then nothing has to be considered a failure... unless, of course, we stop there.

This quote is important in terms of attitude and mindset. A good coach requires the ability to motivate others and this is possible only if you can keep your enthusiasm, even when things are not perhaps going according to plan.

The command and control approach to management is dead!

Long live a coaching approach.

Although the title of "manager" is a generic one which may encompass a very wide range of jobs within an even wider range of organizational settings, managers, on the whole, are responsible for two key aspects:

1.   Ensuring that the actual "work" (whatever that may be) gets done

And

2.   Developing the potential and getting the most out of individual team members.

In the past the job of manager was often based upon the idea of showing direct reports exactly what to do and telling them precisely how to do it.

A few basic problems with the command and control approach.

* It relies on the manager having personal first-hand experience of every job their direct reports undertake. In the past this may well have been the case, where a manager became a manger by being good at a particular job and working their way up an organization's hierarchy. However, more often than not these days, managers have not actually done the jobs of those they are managing and even if they have, the world of work is changing so rapidly that the current job may be unrecognizable from the version the manager once did.

* This approach can break down when the manager is not there in person to supervise (a case of "when the cat's away" syndrome).

* The manager may spend a lot of time taking over operational tasks and fire-fighting.

* This approach does not encourage people to think creatively, develop problem solving abilities or discover their own solutions but rather encourages greater dependence upon the

manager. This can lead to increased stress for the manager, burn-out and overload.

The world of work is moving and changing faster than at any other time in history. Therefore, although as a manager you are probably still responsible for planning and directing the work of a group of individuals, monitoring their work and taking corrective action when necessary, it is unlikely you can do this in the old style of "command and control".

Effective managerial coaching

There are lots of studies that conclude managers who get the most from teams spend a high proportion of their time and energy coaching.

Effective managerial coaches are able to:

★   delegate more

★   create a stronger sense of purpose within the team

★   and motivate the performance of others

Even more important, perhaps, they free up their time so they can focus on the most important tasks, instead of fire-fighting or doing jobs that could be done by direct reports.

"Tell me and I will forget,

show me and I may remember

but involve me and I will understand"

This Chinese proverb could be about the benefits of coaching as a management activity. The old command and control style involves telling direct reports what to do and how to do it. This approach is likely to be met with arguments about how "that won't work" or silent, passive-aggressive non-compliance. Coaching involves the coachee rather than leaving them to be merely a passive recipient of knowledge and direction from the manager. Coachees are supported by the coach to be actively involved in problem solving, decision making and discovering effective solutions to challenges at work.

Overwhelm.

A real problem for managers and leaders.

Against a backdrop of "do more with less" at work and ever increasingly high expectations at home to have everything and do everything just perfectly, it is common to experience overwhelm.

The following are some fairly typical signs of overwhelm:

- Burn-out

- Stress

- High demands on time / on energy

- Feeling unable to cope

- Procrastination / difficulty making decisions

- Work / life balance

- Lack of control

- Focus on what's wrong rather than on what's right (or at least okay!)

- Never quite satisfied with own performance so keep raising the bar

Overwhelm can lead to being active but not productive. Constantly busy but still not getting all the necessary tasks completed. Life is fast-paced with increasing levels of responsibility and pressure for most people in management and leadership roles. Especially in these tough economic times, "restructuring" in reality often means there are fewer people expected to do the same amount of work (or more) with less resources. Even when we are "doing nothing" we seem never to actually be doing nothing.

We live and work in an era of 24/7 input and instant availability. We now consider the multitude of smart technology not merely as a luxury but as an absolute necessity. For many the frantic pace extends into "leisure" time too.

The divide between personal and professional life seems to have become a bit of a blur. In reality we all know that what happens at work impacts on our home life and what happens at home impacts on work. Early bird sessions at the gym, a variety of scheduled activities the kids have to be accompanied to, domestic tasks that require us to be interior designers and Michelin star chefs, more and more opportunities for having a good time can add to the overwhelm of more to do in less time.

A common cry I hear from managers and leaders I coach who are experiencing overwhelm is:

"Everything will be okay when...

I get this piece of work finished

meet this deadline

get the right team

(fill in your own specific phrase)! "

Or sometimes it is:

"Everything would be okay... if I just had more time."

The reality is that there will always be more work than you can complete. In the 21st century, work rarely has a specified finish line or even clear boundaries.

In fact "more time" is rarely the answer to overwhelm because, just like money, if you are not effectively managing what you have, simply having more is not going to make you better at managing.

Parkinson's Law

"Work expands so as to fill the time available for its completion".

It can be easy to think that stress is solely caused by external events, situations, experiences and other people. Yet this is not strictly correct. Research has found that the Transactional Model of Stress is more accurate. This model says that stress is caused by a transaction, that is, there is an interaction between the stressor, our view of the stressor and our perceived ability to cope with it. It is our own internal beliefs, attitudes, interpretations, perceptions and other factors, in combination with the external events that tend to create stress.

Your internal world creates your external world because the way you think and feel about external events will determine how you behave and the actions you take (or avoid). And it is this that creates the results you actually get.

Are you spinning too many plates?

Perhaps you feel that there is no one else who can or will do what needs to be done the way you know it needs to be done?

Well maybe it is true that no one can do the job quite as well as you can. But as you can't do everything all of the time, developing the competence and confidence of the people who report to you will mean that delegation becomes easier rather than a source of stress in itself.

Delegate to empower

The problem with being a good plate spinner is that others will give you their plates to spin too.

As a manager or leader your role is to get things done, not to do it all personally! Coaching your staff can lead to you having a great confidence in their ability to problem solve and make effective decisions. This makes the dreaded "D" word of delegation easier and more effective.

In addition to developing a coaching approach, here are five suggested strategies for tackling overwhelm:

1. Because modern work has no clear finish line and boundaries you need to create these. (Unless you work on an assembly line where this is decided for you, and actually this can create another kind of overwhelm - of not being in control - you will have to.) Set and keep strong boundaries of time and activity by creating start and finish lines for work.

2. Reducing and monitoring your information input and learning how to be with yourself without external stimuli can be useful in reducing a sense of overwhelm. Your mind requires time to process, to do the equivalent of some mental filing.

3. Deciding when, where and to whom you are available.

    Or when to tweet or Facebook and when to opt out!

4.   Making a commitment to clear clutter. Your external world (even your desk) is a reflection of your internal world. Are you hanging on to stuff that is unnecessary, just in case? This behaviour is often fear-driven. The fear of what if I need something I haven't got?

5.   Accept that it is simply not possible to ever get everything done! (Especially trying to do it all yourself.)

Delegating effectively to staff you have developed via coaching so that you are confident in their abilities, will mean you can stop working harder to achieve less. And can focus on what you do best; being a manager and leader.

Developing your coaching approach

If you hold a management position the chances are one of the expectations of your role now is that you will "coach" your direct reports in order to improve their performance, increase their motivation etc. But what exactly is "coaching" and how do you go about doing it on a day-to-day basis?

The following sections provide you with simple, practical and straightforward assistance in developing a coaching approach:

★ with those you manage, to enhance their performance, competence and confidence. Developing better teams of people who report to you will be good for them and great for you as it will reduce your stress levels and experience of overwhelm.

★ you can apply aspects of the model to yourself so that in effect you can be your own coach. This is really useful as it provides you with a structured perspective to work through issues. If you are a manager or leader there are, of course, always significant benefits to working with a professional coach who is external to your organization. Because they are outside of the culture of your organization, they can illuminate your blind spots for you and they are likely to push you to go that little bit beyond what you think you are capable of!

Have you noticed that the world of coaching loves an acronym?

Many other books on coaching are overflowing with acronyms: GROW, ARROW, TGROW, OSKAR, ACHIEVE, CLEAR... This list goes on and on. Now, while these can be useful tools to help you remember your way through a process, the problem with acronyms is that in order to make a process fit the acronym neatly, it usually necessitates omitting essential elements of the process itself. Thereby, in an attempt to make the process simpler or to use words whose first letter sits neatly within the chosen acronym, some of the very substance of the process itself is lost.

Sometimes the actual meaning of a chosen word that fits the acronym is in fact slightly spurious in relation to the step it represents. This often means that the coach has to second guess what to do during that particular step. A classic example of this is in the GROW model.

The GROW model is a very widely used behavioural coaching model which was developed by Graham Alexander and made popular by Sir John Whitmore. In GROW the R relates to the section of the model where the current situation is explored in relation to the desired Goal. Which is the G of the model. However, because the R in this acronym stands for the word "Reality" I have witnessed many coaches incorrectly use this step to assess the reality of the goal itself. If this is done at this early stage in a coaching process it is likely that the limiting beliefs, of potentially both or either the coach and coachee, concerning what is in fact possible, will take over and totally sabotage the coaching process. This can be very demotivating for the coachee who may even feel foolish to have such an "unrealistic" goal let alone express it to a coach!

In light of all of this I made a conscious decision not to even attempt to give the following framework a catchy acronym. In this section I offer what I believe to be a useful, concise and practical "How to coach" framework. It is presented in a way that makes logical sense. Like steps or rungs on a ladder it will help you to help the person you are coaching get from where they currently are to where they aspire to be.

In terms of coaching, I believe that the analogy of a ladder is a useful one because, just as the following Chinese proverb states:

"It is better to take many small steps in the right direction than to make a great leap forward only to stumble backward."

When we are planning to make changes to some aspect of our life or striving towards a new aspiration, it is important to be aware of not falling into the trap of overestimating what can be done in the short term. If we do overestimate what is possible in the short term we are in danger of not achieving what we thought we would. This can result in feeling disheartened and losing the initial motivation and enthusiasm for the goal. We may perhaps even give up on the project altogether.

The flip side of this is that, in fact, we underestimate just how much can be done in the long run. Even if we are making only what appear to be small but consistent changes.

If you wanted to get physically fit for instance, there would be little long-lasting benefit in rushing to the gym today and enthusiastically throwing yourself into a tough workout that you do only once. However, if you follow a reasonable regime consistently then over time you will enjoy the benefits of, and notice the difference in, your fitness levels.

If a large ocean liner makes even a slight adjustment to its navigational course, even one that is so small it is imperceptible in the short term, it will in the long term alter the ultimate destination at which it arrives.

In these days of the promise of on-the-spot solutions, quick fixes and the quest for instant gratification there exists an illusion that short-term pleasure is a substitute for the longer term rewards of genuine fulfilment and satisfaction gained from doing a good job, well.

We may think that just because we can see where we are and identify where we want to be, that should be sufficient to achieve it.

We may get frustrated that we can't do it in one leap from the bottom of the ladder to the top.

However, just like the rungs on a ladder, if we take it one step at a time, be persistent and just keep going, getting to the top is a foregone conclusion.

While the person who is still jumping up and down at ground level bemoaning the fact that they "should" or "ought" to be where they want to be simply because they know where that is, will stay stuck and increasingly exasperated.

Like it or not (and believe me I know it may not be a particularly sexy notion!), but in the future we all reap the consequences of the actions we take or avoid taking in the present. This is why coaching is so powerful and empowering because it focuses on action. To be more specific, the actions you can start taking, based on where you are and what you have. It focuses on the empowering idea that you are not a victim of circumstances, because no matter what has happened to you, or what you have missed out on, it is not the circumstances of life that define you. But rather it is what you choose to do with those circumstances.

"I can't change the direction of the wind, but I can adjust my sails to always reach my destination."

Jimmy Dean

The   Hummingbird   Effect Coaching Framework

W hy "The Hummingbird Effect"? Well it is a play on the term "The Butterfly Effect" which refers to the idea that the sedate flapping of a butterfly's wings might create tiny changes in the atmosphere that could ultimately alter the path of a tornado. The flapping wing represents a small change in the initial condition of the system, which causes a chain of events leading to large scale alterations of events. Well, hummingbirds can flap their wings at up to 100 beats per second. Hummingbirds also symbolize flexibility, being the only birds that can fly in all directions. In relation to coaching we have already established that it is the small changes that ultimately create significant change. Flexibility is crucial in order to constantly assess if the actions that are being taken are having the desired result, that is getting the coachee closer to their goal or destination or not? Flexibility is required to make necessary adjustments. It is utterly pointless to keep doing the same thing over and over, to be rigid in approach and expect the results you are getting to just miraculously be different.

The Hummingbird Effect Coaching Framework

Step One

Establish the REASON for coaching

This might seem like common sense.

But have you noticed that common sense does not necessarily equate to common practice?

Establish what the reason or subject matter is for the session.

Without clear, mutually agreed and understood guidelines for what the coaching is actually about it is unlikely to produce any specific or measurable rewards for anyone.

In a classic coaching scenario it would always be the coachee who decides this. However, in a real world work situation where you are using a coaching approach as a manager or leader the topic may be externally decided. For instance, the coaching may be required as a way to address a performance issue that has come to light.

Or the coaching may form a part of the ongoing personal and professional development of the coachee.

Or there may be some other overall purpose which might determine or at least influence the initial reason for coaching.

The key to success here is that the reason for the coaching needs to be mutually agreed and explicitly understood by both you as the coach and the person you are coaching.

Otherwise the coaching session could end up like one of those excruciating comedies of errors where people appear to be communicating but in fact are at cross purposes.

Step Two

Set the SCOPE of the coaching

What is the scope and/or any boundaries of the session?

This is commonly known in coaching as "contracting".

Not to be confused with any type of administrative contract there may be in place.

Again the key to success at this step is to mutually agree and understand what the session will (and in some cases, what it will not) encompass.

Certain limitations may be dictated by external factors such as the time available, the number of sessions permitted, or by the necessity to focus on an element of a larger issue.

Perhaps a restriction is placed on the coaching by an organization that only directly work-related issues are deemed appropriate for consideration or discussion within a coaching session.

Attempting to separate completely any personal issues from work-related issues can, in practice, be extremely difficult. We are human beings and not merely work machines and, therefore, what happens in our personal lives impacts directly on our ability to perform adequately at work. And vice versa. Sometimes, even if the reason for the coaching is very firmly rooted in work, it may be something in the coachee's personal life that needs to be addressed.

During my time coaching within organizations, I have had many experiences of this. Here are just two examples:

I was engaged to coach a highly regarded, very able, senior manager. She had a recent history of suffering from severe stress/burn-out. In the past she had been forced to take time off sick at very short notice and her company were concerned that she was heading for another "breakdown". During our initial discussions it became apparent that while her job was extremely demanding, she was eminently capable and had a good team around her.

She soon confided that it was not work but rather relationship problems which was causing her increased stress.

She went on to reveal that her marriage had been dysfunctional for a long time but because of various reasons she had kept this a secret from those she worked with. So none of her colleagues or managers knew anything about how difficult the challenges she was facing at home were.

Her husband had recently moved out leaving her to cope alone with all the domestic responsibilities, childcare arrangements and the task of trying to sell the family home. She was dealing with many sources of stress in her personal life which, of course, were having an impact on her performance at work. But work was not in itself the problem. So therefore the focus of the coaching became supporting her to resolve the practicalities and emotional impact of her personal situation. This had the desired effect of reducing her stress levels and there was a positive impact on her performance at work.

If her organization had put a restriction around the subject matter of the sessions to specify we should tackle only directly professional issues then the coaching would not have achieved the actual intended purpose. Which was for this organization to support a senior employee and prevent her from "breaking down".

The second example concerned another senior manager in a different organization whose performance at work had suddenly and drastically deteriorated. It transpired the reason was because he had been having a long-term extra marital affair with a colleague in his team. She had recently decided to end the relationship and he was finding the whole situation really difficult to manage.

Again, if we had been prevented from exploring aspects of his personal as well as his professional life within the coaching, in my opinion it would have been impossible to coach him effectively.

Step Three

Agree the OUTCOME for the session

What is the desired outcome for the specific session?

There is a need to be practical and reasonable about what can actually be achieved within a single session.

A way to do this is by keeping steps one and two in mind, and then discovering what is it that the coachee wants to walk away with at the end of this particular session.

What is it they want to come out of the session with?

Coachees should also be mindful of not over-planning a session based on what was covered in the previous one. Coaches need to be fully prepared, but mindful that things change between sessions. As do priorities. It is therefore a good idea at the start of each session to clearly establish the outcome for that particular session.

The first three steps

Steps one, two and three are interrelated and therefore in some coaching models they are grouped under one heading. However, in my experience, separating them and establishing them as discrete steps ensures that all the bases are adequately covered and therefore it is less likely that anything gets forgotten or inadvertently omitted.

Goal Setting

Beware, the following can seem complicated!

A popular acronym associated with goal setting is SMART.

Yes, another acronym!

SMART represents the various aspects of goal setting which are most likely to lead to the successful achievement of a stated goal.

S is for specific.

That is, ensure you say what you want rather than what you don't want. Ensure you are precise about describing what the goal actually is.

M is for measurable.

It is important to establish how you will actually know when you have achieved the goal. What will be your evidence? What will be different?

A is for achievable or attainable.

Is it possible for a human being to achieve this goal? What is involved in achieving it?

R is for realistic.

Is it realistic for you, given where you are now and your time-frame, resources etc. Sometimes R is for relevant. How does the goal fit with all aspects of your life? Is it really relevant to you or just something you think you should want?

T is for timed.

In order to ensure that things get done there needs to be an established timetable of what needs to be done when.

Add an E for Emotions and SMART becomes SMARTE

In other words how do you feel about the goal? Excited, motivated, inspired, terrified?

How will it feel to achieve the goal?

The addition of the E is because it is, in fact, emotion (rather than just logic alone) that actually gets us moving.

And just for good measure how about adding:

I for Insight / Intuition / or Instinct?

What is the sum of your knowledge, experience and gut feeling telling you about the goal? What can bringing these into the equation add?

Extending the acronym to SMARTIE!

What about long, medium and short term goals?

These could be thought of as chronological stepping stones that lead you nicely from where you are to where you want to be.

I once heard that many people experience disappointment, not due to the fact that they dream too big and fail, but that they dream too small and succeed in achieving those small dreams!

Thinking and dreaming big, deciding on the ultimate reason and purpose for an outcome is what generates enough motivation to do what needs to be done.

Goals need to be linked to a greater purpose and have significant meaning for the coachee, otherwise it is unlikely they will be actioned, let alone accomplished.

"Dreams are the seeds of change.

Nothing ever grows without a seed,

and nothing ever changes without a dream."

Debby Boone

Step Four

Assess the CURRENT SITUATION

This step is about exploring the current situation in relation to the goal. What is their current reality compared to their desired reality, the desired reality being how things will be once they have achieved the goal?

When comparing the specific details of the current situation to the desired situation there can be a tendency for coachees to see things in very global, generalized terms. In other words exaggerating the gap between the two.

The coach should aim for a true exploration of how the coachee perceives the current situation. Once this is established the coach can go on to challenge this in order to separate the facts from the coachee's beliefs and opinions.

This step in itself is often very useful to the coachee.

Celebrate

This step also provides an important opportunity to celebrate any successes and appreciate what the coachee has already achieved on their way to the goal. Even if this is, in fact, no more than that they have worked to establish some clarity around what the goal is, what they are aiming for. This is important because how can you improve your aim in order to hit a target until you actually identify what the target is?

Many people do not get what they want from life, mainly because they don't ever decide what it is that they actually want. Therefore, even if this is "all" the coachee has done so far, they are way ahead of many others.

Confidence is crucial

There have been studies that show there is a direct correlation between the confidence the coach has in the coachee and the coachee's achievements.

> *"Confidence is contagious.*
>
> *So is the lack of it."*
>
> *Vince Lombardi*

Do not, however, patronize your coachee.

The empty cry of "good job" at every opportunity (said in a mid-Atlantic accent, of course, and possibly accompanied by a high-five) is demeaning to all.

It is the acknowledgement of real competence and credibility which creates genuine confidence. Just as experience begets expertise. You don't become an expert just because you say you are, but rather only because others regard you as such.

Over-inflated or unfounded confidence is merely delusion and can create more problems than it solves.

True confidence and recognition in genuine ability is a beneficial element to achievement. Because what prevents many people from achieving their goals isn't lack of skill, ability or potential to do what they want to do, but rather it is a lack of confidence to even try.

"Whatever you believe with feeling becomes your reality."

Brian Tracy

This step provides the honest exploration and understanding of the current "location" of the coachee. This is necessary in order to plan the most appropriate route to the desired "destination". This plan is created by the following steps.

Step Five

Explore all the available CHOICES.

This is where all the possible ways to get from current "location" to desired "destination" are considered.

During this step there are no limits.

Everything is up for consideration in terms of:

What could be done?

What might be done?

What others would do?

What could be done that the coachee would never usually consider?

Choices, what choices?

It is not unusual for coachees to express the belief that they have no choice. Or that their choices are severely limited. However, the simple truth is that we always have choices; we just might not like them!

No matter what happens, we always have a choice. Even when it seems that there is no option, there is always something else that can be done. And ultimately what happens in our lives is the result of decisions that we make. In fact, in every situation we ALWAYS have at least two choices:

1.   To do something

   And

2.   To not do something

It is empowering for the coachee to appreciate that they are making choices rather than feeling forced into a situation or course of action.

During this step the coach should aim to gently but firmly push the coachee beyond perhaps what they would normally consider possible for them.

This step is not about coming up with just the ONE RIGHT answer.

It is about considering all the possible options that could potentially be taken.

At this stage do not permit the coachee to criticise any of the options or put up an argument about how they "won't work because…"

A crucial element of coaching is getting the balance of support and challenge just right.

This step is an opportunity for the coach to encourage and support the coachee in exploring ideas and to challenge them to go further and think of even more options.

Step Six

Assess the potential CONSEQUENCES of each choice.

This is where the coach can encourage the coachee to play devil's advocate and be really ultra-critical in order to fully explore all the arguments against or all the reasons why particular options might not be suitable.

The idea is not to reject all the options out of hand, but rather by establishing potential obstacles and then going on to identify how to overcome these and successfully implementing them, the range of potential available options will be narrowed down.

So once the coachee has identified the obstacles get them to identify ways in which these barriers to success could potentially be overcome.

This step is often a very dynamic and creative part of the coaching process.

"By prevailing over all obstacles and distractions, one may unfailingly arrive at his chosen goal or destination."

Christopher Columbus

Step Seven

DECISION TIME

"In any moment of decision, the best thing you can do is the right thing,

the next best thing is the wrong thing,

and the worst thing you can do is nothing."

Theodore Roosevelt

Having fully explored all the options, the potential problems and how to solve these, it is now decision time.

As a result of step six it is likely that clear favourites would have emerged. Often these are significantly different and far from the options that the coachee would have imagined prior to the coaching session.

Step seven is concerned with establishing what the coachee will really do out of all the possible things they have identified they could do.

Often making a firm decision about what to actually do in order to achieve a goal or outcome is in itself very motivating.

This creates a very real sense that they are on their way.

"Once you make a decision, the universe conspires to make it happen."

Ralph Waldo Emerson

Step Eight

AGREE ACTIONS

This step follows on from the previous one because once the coachee has decided what option(s) they are going to choose, in order to maximize the possibility for success and minimize the potential for them to get sidetracked, once they are away from the coaching environment, a plan of action is necessary.

You could use the SMARTIE framework to assist the coachee to get to the specifics of this.

Identifying the "What are you going to do?" and "When are you going to do it?" provides criteria for measurable evidence.

The danger of "I'll get it done by the end of next week" syndrome.

Although this type of statement sounds specific, in fact it is quite vague because it doesn't specify when "the end" actually is.

Plus, if no starting point is established, they may waste a lot of time and energy unproductively putting the task off until the last minute. If this happens there is more danger of something else taking priority and getting in the way.

"A real decision is measured by the fact that you've taken a new action.

If there's no action, you haven't truly decided."

Tony Robbins

Step Nine

ACCOUNTABILITY

As coach (and manager) the coachee is logically accountable to you as the coach (and manager). However, there may be additional or alternative systems of accountability that can be utilized in order to increase the coachee's motivation.

For instance, being answerable to sub-teams, reporting to meetings or particular colleagues etc.

Obviously some form of accountability is essential otherwise, no matter how well-intentioned, they might get distracted from the process.

Nothing gets done without a deadline. And a deadline is only a deadline if you have to report back to someone else!

"People tend not to just wander around and then find themselves at the top of Mount Everest."

Zig Ziglar

Step Ten

PLANNING TO REVIEW

Having a schedule for review is a necessary part of the ongoing process of coaching. Otherwise it would not truly differ much from merely sending the coachee away with a "to do" list of instructions to carry out.

Even in the very best "text book" case of following this step-by-step coaching process the reality of what happens as a result of what the coachee does may not be what was anticipated.

Review is a valuable way of assessing performance and results in order to gain essential feedback in order to either take remedial action or plan further improvements.

Experience is what you get when you don't get what you expected!

TOTE

The whole process of coaching could be slotted into the TOTE model. The TOTE model was developed in the 1960s by psychologists Eugene Galanter, Karl Pribram and George Armitage Miller.

The model describes and explains human behaviour and expands on the Stimulus Response model of Ivan Pavlov which describes behaviour in terms of conditioning. That is, a response results from a stimulus. In NLP, TOTES are used to explore strategies.

The TOTE acronym (yes I know, another one... but to be fair there haven't been THAT many in this book now have there?) is:

T = Test

O = Operate

T = Test

E = Exit

Anything we do will involve a *TOTE.*

Test = comparison between what we want and what we have

Operate = do something to close the gap

Test = did the action you took get you to where you want to be?

Yes?

Exit

No?

Operate = do something more / different etc.

Test again etc.

In order to do the review, a date and time need to be agreed for the next coaching session. The actual review takes place at the beginning of the following session forming part of the theme / contracting / and going on to the outcome stage.

Getting Started

Obviously, while it is neither possible nor desirable to attempt to script a conversation, there follows a list of "starter" questions / statements which give a flavour for each step. This is by no means an exhaustive list. The intention is to get you started on using the framework to coach and help you gain an understanding of what each step in the process is about and how it flows to the next in relation to the whole coaching procedure.

Step One = Reason

If the reason for the coaching is to concentrate on something specific, for instance if a performance issue needs to be addressed, then being explicit about this and ensuring the coachee is fully aware is important.

"I just want to establish that the main purpose for these coaching sessions is to support you in achieving X Y Z"

If the coaching forms part of the ongoing personal and/or professional development of the coachee it may be that the coachee and coach mutually decide on the overall reason.

"This organization recognizes the benefits of coaching in terms of maximizing the potential of staff and so there are various areas we could focus on… (X Y Z) which ones appeal to you, or do you have any other ideas or suggestions?"

Step Two = Scope

The scope and any boundaries may be influenced by things such as:

★ the amount of time, and/or number of sessions available,

★ the range of subject matters that are to be covered,

★ confidentiality and exceptions to this in terms of others who may be privy to information / subject of discussions.

The importance of confirming this is so coach and/or coachee can refer back to it, should the coaching stray too far from the agreed "contract". If this does happen, this step ensures there is a respectful way to get the coaching back on track. Or, if necessary, a way to identify that perhaps a revision of the contract may be required.

"Now we have established the overall purpose of the coaching, it might be useful to establish the scope and any boundaries for the sessions..."

Step Three = Outcome for the Session

Having agreed the overall reason and the scope of the coaching, attention can now be focused on the specific session.

"What do you want to come out of this session?

"What do you want to get from this particular session?"

"If you could leave here at the end of this session with something, what would it be?"

"What would you like to discuss?"

"What do you want instead of the problem / current situation?"

"Given that we have (X amount of time) today, what do you want to talk about?

Step Four = Current Situation

In this step the idea is to evaluate the current situation with regard to the goal.

"Tell me a bit about what is happening at the moment?"

"In relation to (the goal) how close or far are you from it?"

"Explain the current situation, not better not worse, but as it is?"

Step Five = Choices

This step focuses on creating as many varied options and choices as possible.

"Let's brainstorm all the potential ways you could get from where you are, to where you want to be in relation to this (goal)"?

"What could be done?"

"What else? What else?" etc.

"What might someone else do?"

"What would you tell a friend to do in this situation?"

"What are the other options?"

"Tell me something that someone could possibly do, even if you would not do it?"

"Why would you not do it?"

Step Six = Consequences

"Looking at all the possible options you have generated, let's put them in order from most likely to least likely."

"Taking the top 5, what might stop you / get in the way / what might be the problems involved in doing this?"

"How could you overcome these?"

"Do you need support / resources / help?"

"What do you consider to be the pros and cons of each option?"

Denise Collins

Step Seven = Decision Time

Time to make a firm decision.

"Which of the potential choices do you feel committed to / excited by?"

"Out of all of the possibilities, which are you going to choose?"

"What will you do?"

Step Eight = Agree the Actions

"Okay so you have decided to do X Y Z have I got that right?

"Great, so now you have selected, let's create a plan."

"What is the first / easiest/ most useful / smallest step?"

Encourage the coachee to commit to specific days, timescales etc.

Step Nine = Accountability

"As I am coaching you during these sessions it makes sense that I will be checking to see how you have got on... reason for this is to support you... is that okay?

"What other ways can you think of that will ensure you stay committed to the agreed actions?"

"Who else can you make yourself accountable to to ensure you stick to your plan?"

Step Ten = Planning to Review

"Same time next week… then we will start that next session by reviewing what you have done and the results that have been achieved?

"When shall we meet for our next session?"

"In time for our next session (specify a date) please email me a summary of what you have done and the consequences so far. Then we can discuss it in the session."

Incorporating an appreciative approach to coaching

"Appreciative Inquiry" was developed by David Cooperrider. It is based on the notion that organizations change in the direction in which they "inquire". That is, in the direction in which they ask questions and focus attention.

So if an organization inquires into problems it will keep discovering more and more problems. If an organization inquires into what it does well and appreciates what is good, it will discover more and more good practice, success and accomplishment.

It will, as a result, develop a culture where these can be built upon and developed.

These ideas can be effectively and quite simply applied when coaching using what is known as the 4D model as a framework.

Based on the "Appreciative Inquiry" 4D model

1. Discover = appreciate the best of what is

2. Dream = envision desired results. Consider what might be?

3. Design = co–construct "what shall we include in the dream?"

4. Destiny = how do we make it happen? How do we learn, adjust and improve?

1. Discover. The coach helps the coachee reframe the issue in a more positive way:

   "I'm not very good at X part of my job" might become, "How can I get better at X part of my job?"

   Appreciative questions can move the process forward:

   "What parts of your job are you good at?"

   "What would others say you are good at?" and so on.

2. Dream. Having helped the coachee discover the positive core of their work and what they can value about themselves and their ways of working, the coach can help the coachee look to the future:

   "What is your desired future at work?"

"If you could be exactly how you want to be at your job, tell me about that."

"What successes do you see yourself celebrating at work in the future?"

3. Design. This phase involves helping the coachee bring their dreams into clear focus and affirming the reality of the dream. It also involves investigating and supporting the actions needed to bring the dream into being:

    "Thinking about (your dream) what would need to happen for it to come into reality?"

    "What have you done in the past that you could do again to help you move towards (the dream)?"

4. Destiny. It has been said that we are often more afraid of our strengths than our weaknesses. One of the roles of the appreciative coach to is affirm the strengths of their coachee to help them acknowledge and accept these. It may also be necessary to be there for support when things get difficult, as they often will. There is rarely a smooth progression from dream to reality and coachees will often get discouraged. The effective coach

will know how to support without patronizing
or taking over.

Five top tips to stack the odds in favour of success

There has been research which indicates that those people who are successful in terms of their achievement of goals and ambitions share certain common behaviours. During part of the coaching process it can be helpful to share these with your coachee.

Tip 1.

Create a step-by-step plan.

> *"A good plan is like a road map: it shows the final destination and usually the best way to get there."*
>
> H. Stanley Judd

Tip 2.

Go public.

This relates to accountability.

"Accountability breeds response-ability."

Stephen R. Covey

Tip 3.

Establish the benefits.

In other words, life has to be better in some way or why bother to make a change?

Tip 4.

Celebrate success.

Ensure that the achievement of each step along the way is rewarded.

The reward must not, of course, conflict with the overall goal. A classic example of an interim reward that is in conflict with the ultimate goal would be to be rewarded for a "good week" of dieting by having a big cream cake!

Celebrating success at each step increases a sense of achievement and encourages further motivation to continue. A "well done" for what has been achieved is far more powerful for most people that an admonishment for any shortcomings.

"Nothing succeeds like success."

Oscar Wilde

Tip 5.

Write it down.

Some say that in order to increase ownership, it is essential that it is the coachee who must do the writing. So long as everything is mutually agreed and understood, I believe it is less relevant to success, who holds the pen.

"Don't just think it, ink it."

A word about motivation…

As a manager, leader and/or coach you may be expected to be a source of motivation for others.

Unfortunately, motivation is not a substance that can be poured into others like petrol can be poured into a car!

I have been really amused by seeing coaches who appear to be trying to "infect" their coachees with motivation and enthusiasm by playing a role akin to Tigger after too many espressos.

The real role of the coach is to discover and establish how the goal or desired outcome is meaningful and has purpose for the person undertaking it.

All too often a mistake that is made is to use your own criteria for attempting to motivate others, rather than actually discovering what theirs are.

Unless you do discover how the goal or outcome has meaning and purpose and is important to the person undertaking it, their commitment will be less and any motivation you can muster will be extrinsic.

Explore what is important to the coachee in the realm of the goal or outcome. Explore how they will benefit (e.g. in terms of feeling fulfilled by the achievement) from accomplishing the goal or outcome. Explore the broader meaning of this for them and what it might then enable them to do.

Once you have an understanding of this, it becomes easier to motivate because it involves a process of linking what is important and meaningful to them to the achievement of the goal or outcome.

Know the boundaries.

Emotional distress, psychological disorders and coaching.

As a coaching manager you need to be aware of the potential limitations and appropriateness of coaching as an intervention. In other words, you need to know when not to coach those who report to you. Coaching is a powerful way to enhance skill, competence and confidence, and to deal effectively with performance issues and general professional (and personal) development. And even though there will often be an overlap between personal and professional issues, as previously mentioned in terms of establishing boundaries during the setting the scope step, coaching is not appropriate for helping people to overcome severe emotional distress, psychological disorders and/or mental health issues.

Depression is now the number one psychological disorder in the western world. At the current rate of increase, it is expected to become the second most disabling condition in the world by 2020 (behind only heart disease). Therefore, it is highly likely that a significant number of the people who report to you will experience depression and may even be undergoing medical treatment for it.

Workplace coaching, no matter how good, is not a therapeutic intervention. It is important that you have adequate sources to refer to should you get "out of your depth" with the problems or issues presented to you by a coachee. You may inadvertently do more harm than good if you attempt to use coaching inappropriately with someone whose issues are beyond the scope of what you as a coaching manager can deal with. No matter how well-intentioned you are or how great a desire you have to help a coachee, it could also be disheartening and demotivating for you to attempt to deal with something that requires therapy rather than coaching.

That is not to say that you cannot coach people who have experienced trauma in the past. Or people who have been diagnosed with depression, or show the signs or symptoms of being depressed. In fact, given the statistics on depression, it would be hard to avoid. It is just that you should not attempt to coach them on the subject of the trauma or depression.

A possible exception would be if you have suitable training and a background as a professional therapist. Plus the blessing of your organization to undertake this role within a coaching-at-work context.

There is growing interest among coaches who also have training and skill in therapy, and therapists who undertake additional training in coaching, to develop an integrated service which is sometimes known as personal consultancy. However, at least for the moment, this is not widely offered within a coaching-at-work setting. In order to protect both the coach and coachee, the manager who wants to adopt a coaching approach should be aware of operating within appropriate boundaries.

Conclusions

If you are one of the many leaders or managers who struggle to do everything that needs to be done in less time and with fewer resources I thank you for investing your precious time in reading this book. The proof of how beneficial the ideas and coaching framework offered here in this book are in helping to motivate and improve the performance of your teams, will be discovered only by adopting them. It is only by using them that you can truly assess their worth in terms of improving the competence, responsibility, confidence, problem solving and effective decision making skills of those people who report to you.

If your professional role includes the expectation that you will coach, I sincerely hope this book increases your feelings of competence to do so effectively. I would appreciate feedback on your experiences of using The Hummingbird Effect Coaching Framework with those who report to you.

Remember:

Change is inevitable.

Progress and improvement are optional.

"The only thing constant in life is change."

François de la Rochefoucauld

The world of work is constantly changing. The rate of that change is getting ever more rapid. Whether your inclination is to resist it, embrace it or maybe just to tolerate it, choice about change is not an option. We all know that change is inevitable. Whatever we do, even if we do nothing, things still change. Progress and improvement, however, are optional.

"It is not the strongest of the species that survive, nor the most intelligent, but the one most responsive to change."

Charles Darwin

Improving your performance as a coach

Learn.

Practise.

Continue learning.

Continue to practise what you learn.

The more you practise the more you will improve.

The more you improve, the better the results you will get.

The better the results you achieve, the more you will want to practise and the better you will get.

Whatever happened today,

good, bad or indifferent,

there is always tomorrow.

"Tomorrow is the most important thing in life. It comes into us at midnight very clean. It's perfect when it arrives and puts itself in our hands. It hopes we've learned something from yesterday"

John Wayne

No matter how busy you are, do what you can today.

Take action and then reflect on your performance.

Seek feedback on the results of your actions.

Learn and strive to improve so that tomorrow what you do is even better than what you did today.

"Tomorrow is another whole new day,

not even started on yet."

Thomas Kennett (my dad)

Looking for practical, professional, independently-approved training?

If you:

* are looking to add skills that are significantly useful in both your professional and personal life,

* have an interest in a variety of ways to develop, support and help yourself and others,

* know a bit about NLP and/or coaching and want to know more,

* feel it is important to you to attend independently-approved useful training

then please check out The Hummingbird Effect open training programmes in:

Eclectic Life and Business Coaching

Recognized by The Association for Coaching and

Approved by The Institute of Leadership and Management as a Development Programme.

NLP Practitioner

Accredited by The Association for NLP

NLP Master Practitioner

Accredited by The Association for NLP

For up-to-date details and special offers visit
www.hummingbirdeffect.com

Looking for corporate training and development for your organization that continues to add value long after the event?

Visit www.hummingbirdeffect.com for information on:

Bespoke development programmes and the current range of in-house programmes including:

★   Being an inspiring and effective leader

★   Creating an effective coaching culture

★   Practical coaching for managers

★   Coaching at work, that works!

★   Confidence, inside and out

★   Presentation skills

★   Time management

★   Stress management

★   The art of training

★ NLP at work

★ Enhancing customer service

★ Building more effective teams

Visit www.hummingbirdeffect.com

Or call:

01245 476376

Do you want to learn from your past, improve your present and create the future you truly desire?

Denise now works with only a select few clients on a one-to-one basis. Utilizing a synthesis of integrated therapeutic coaching and development approaches, she helps people to be the best they can be.

If you want to enhance what you already do well and identify, clarify and achieve what you want from your personal and professional life please get in touch to find out about her availability to see you on an individual basis.

Visit www.hummingbirdeffect.com to discover how individual consultancy can help you.

Or to speak with Denise call 01245 476376